Cooking

WITH

WHOLEGRAINS

BY

ELLEN and VREST ORTON

Introduction by VREST ORTON

Gramercy Publishing Company
New York

Designed by Vrest Orton

This 1982 edition published by Gramercy Publishing Company,
distributed by Crown Publishers, Inc.,
by arrangement with Farrar, Straus & Giroux, Inc.

MANUFACTURED IN THE UNITED STATES OF AMERICA.

ISBN: 0-517-36834X

h g f e d c b a

Library of Congress Cataloging in Publication Data

Orton, Ellen, 1911–
Cooking with wholegrains.

Includes index.
1. Cookery (Cereals) 2. Baking. I. Orton, Vrest,
1897–   . II. Title.
TX808.07   1982   641.6′31   81-20169
                                        AACR2

Contents

The Mystery of the Mill 5

Bread & Rolls 17

Quick Breads, Steamed Breads & Doughnuts 28

Muffins, Popovers & Gems................................ 34

Biscuits, Griddlecakes, Scones & Dumplings 39

Luncheon & Supper Dishes 47

Desserts & Cereals...................................... 51

Index... 63

Mystery of the Mill

"And when I have broken the staff of your bread—
Ye shall eat and not be satisfied."

I

 COOKING BOOK devoted exclusively to cooking with
wholegrain flour is such an old idea that it's brand new.
Up to 1850 there was no other kind of cooking book.
Yet there is probably not in print today, and certainly
there has not been published this side of three-quarters of a century,
a book of this character. This paradox can be best explained by
a brief excursion into the history of milling.

But before this excursion into the past, I must define my terms.
What is this *wholegrain* that we have all heard so much talk about
in the last few years, particularly during the last war? The answer
is simple enough . . . it is *all of* the grain kernel ground into meal
or flour, whether it be corn, rye, wheat or oats.

Some confusion arises due to the several names given the *wholegrain* wheat product. In England, it is variously called wholemeal,
entire wheat, wholegrain, and whole wheaten flour and in America,
Graham flour and "wholewheat" flour. I prefer the term *wholegrain*
flour to distinguish from that now prostituted word *wholewheat*,
which in America has no more meaning whatsoever due to the

shrewd manipulation of the English language by the millers and bakers or their advertising agents. For *wholewheat* is no longer a word meaning *all of* the wheat berry. You can buy "wholewheat" bread and "wholewheat" flour but you are in no sense getting *all of* the kernel of wheat. The millers and bakers get around the federal laws under which manufacturers are supposed to attach true names descriptive of their products by claiming that their product is wholewheat or, in their language, all wheat . . . that is to say, no barley, no corn, no oats. But in no sense is it all *of* the wheat.

Now when and why did the millers, already characterized as shrewd, begin to use less than all of the wheat berry which nature in its munificence furnished to mankind?

II

The story begins in the Stone Age when wheat berries were crushed or pounded between stones by the females of the tribe. After a few thousand years they learned to use saddle-stones, or one concave stone upon which the grain was spread and another stone to rub or grind the grain into a coarse and primitive meal. Even today in Mexico this saddle-stone, called the *metata* there, is used for grinding corn from which the Mexicans make their tortillas. The third and last development of the stone was the *quern* or the stone rotation mill, the first complete milling machine. In existence as early as the second century B.C. this device was composed of two round French Buhr, or granite stones into which grooves were cut (the top turning on the stationary bottom stone), and it persisted down to about 75 years ago in England and America, and indeed is found in back country regions even today.

All of these aforementioned processes obviously ground *all of* the kernel of corn, rye, oats, or wheat into meal, taking no part out and therefore giving real meaning to the word *wholegrain*. Then came the revolution.

About the middle of the 19th Century when the industrial age was reaching out for more production and a mass market, there was invented and developed (chiefly by Hungarians at first and later by other continental Europeans) the roller-mill. The first complete automatic roller-mill was established in the United Kingdom in 1878 at Dublin, although the principle had been introduced into Scotland as early as 1872.

The roller-mill, ancestor of the contemporary milling apparatus in practically all civilized countries, consisted principally of a pair of fluted or grooved metal rollers. Unlike the single pair of cold stones turned slowly by waterpower, these rollers were arranged in a series, beginning with breakers to split the wheat, thus releasing the starch or endosperm so that it might be completely pulverized and ground by the smoother reduction rollers into the white flour we know today. Naturally speed was the main objective. Such a system produced flour just about 100 times faster than the old slow-poke stone mills.

Yet the very slowness of the stone mill constituted its chief value as a food producing tool. The rich germ of the grain kernel is volatile and susceptible to rancidity when heated in grinding, and if so heated clogs up the grinding surfaces. But the cold stone mills turned slowly, and could pulverize the germ into the flour or meal. But like many another tool of earlier days, character and quality soon became less important than speed, and so the stone mills gave way, about 1870, to another machine.

III

Now we come to the "mystery of the mill." What else did the new high-speed steel roller-mill do except to grind grain 100 times faster? Well, it was soon evident that the germ gummed up the high speed rollers. Therefore, by a series of graduated siftings it was possible to screen out this germ. This epoch-making discovery allowed the millers to expedite their operations, but more significant, they discovered soon enough that flour from which the live and perishable germ was screened out would keep indefinitely on store shelves.

It is rather appalling to realize how easily the milling trade has succeeded these many years keeping these facts from the public, both in America and Great Britain. We only have to look to that famous authority, *The Encyclopedia Britannica*, to obtain bonafide evidence. The erudite and technical account of milling in that compendium was written by an English miller, and it is revealing to see how nonchalantly he treats of the process by which the germ was eliminated. He says, ". . . in roller milling the germ was *easily* separated from the rest of the berry and it was *readily* sifted from the stock. The germ contains a good deal of *fatty matter* which, if allowed to remain, would not increase the keeping qualities of the flour." (The italics are mine.)

That such a standard reference should allow truth to be so distorted is amazing enough, were it not for the more sinister fact that the milling trade has now reached the apotheosis of their craft when they believe their own lies· and perpetuate them with no moral guilt whatever.

But it might be interesting to ask what this refined white flour that *keeps* better is doing to our stomachs. No one has summed it up more succinctly than Geoffrey Bowles in that delightful magazine the British *Countryman*, when he declared: "Much of our national illness is caused by crazes for food that is (1) white, (2) refined, and (3) keepable. All three crazes are exemplified in white flour. The best food chemists are the earth and the sun, which produce the wholewheat that the steel rollers of the white flour millers spoil. White flour makes white faces . . . food is stuff to be eaten fresh, not to be 'kept' as if it were an heirloom . . . wholemeal flour naturally does not 'keep' because the germ in it is alive. Germless white flour 'keeps' because it is dead, because it is as dead as Portland cement powder, all its original goodness having been sifted out of it. Let them 'keep' their flour who have no care to keep their health."

IV

Let it not be thought from the foregoing that our cooking book is a polemic against the milling business. But to understand what actually has happened to food during the years of "refinement," it is necessary to look carefully into that simple thing; the wheat berry or the corn kernel, and to understand why it has been treated so unfairly by men who naturally wish (human nature being what it is) to get out of them not the most nourishment but the most profit.

Without getting too technical we can say that the wheat berry consists of three sections, (a) the skin or what is commonly known as the bran, which holds the rest of the kernel together, (b) the endosperm, in volume the main part of the berry, consisting mostly of tasteless starch and (c) the germ, embryo, or seed of life from which new life springs if planted, and which gives life-nourishing factors if eaten. This energizing germ contains most of the vitamins and minerals of the berry, very approximately 90%. Yet this germ, in modern milling, is cast aside as a by-product. That such a paradox could persist these 75 years seems astonishing. Yet it is easy to see that when a process like modern milling engages an investment of billions of dollars and results in millions of dollars of profit yearly, the millers are not likely to change in favor of producing a better product when they can make more money with what they are doing.

And it is not because they have been given no opportunity. From a process introduced about 1910, down to the revolutionary milling methods of an engineer named Earle, introduced in England before the last war, the millers have been offered machines by which they could not only include the vital germ of the grain in flour, but they could still grind it as fast as by the roller-mill system. Their argument that, to grind the germ into the flour, they would have to return to the stone mill, does not hold water.

The British *Countryman*, at the beginning of the second World War, started a brave crusade for real wholegrain bread in England, but it was not strong enough to beat down the resistance of entrenched business. In this country there has been no concerted movement to oppose the milling trust, and certainly this author is not foolhardy to undertake what would be at best a quixote adventure. However, this is not to say that in the United States there is not an increasing number of persons discovering the truth about modern milling. And certainly in our small hill village in Vermont we have seen what can happen when intelligent people catch on. The 150-year-old Buhr stone mill in Weston is now hard at work grinding daily by waterpower several wholegrain products which are distributed to Americans all over the land by mail.

This wholegrain "revival" is small and will probably never reach more than a million people, because—as authorities have pointed out, there seems to be a perversity in human beings to like things that are not good for them! This is due somewhat to the obdurate fact that the milling and baking groups have for fifty or more years kept alive the public's opinion that refined white flour was refined in more than the technical way, that is, it was socially incorrect to be caught eating dark bread or, as the propagandists now call it, *peasant bread*. Although millions of people today eat· what they assume to be wholewheat bread issued by modern bakers, this is in most cases made of nothing more than patent white flour colored with bran.

The original meaning of the word *flour*, from the French *fleur*, signified "the best part," but it apparently is no longer the best part at all. Even the U. S. Department of Agriculture in one of its Bulletins had the courage to state that ". . . experiments have shown that in general the highly refined flours contain practically none of the vitamins present in the whole grain product."

V

A great to-do has been made in recent years over the "enrichment" of bread and flour. In England millers and bakers were compelled by the government to give the people of that country more vitamins per loaf during the war by producing a higher extraction flour, fortified with synthetic vitamins. However, this very slight improvement was fought bitterly by the millers and bakers who played up the horrible fact that the good folk of England were being *forced* to eat peasant bread! Yet in America, these gentlemen eagerly accepted the enrichment idea, as a sop to public demand for better bread.

But this enrichment program is at bottom a delusion and a deceit.*

The original wheat berry contains a number of minerals such as calcium, iron, and phosphorus as well as fat, and the vitamins A, E, and the B-complex group of vitamins. In the wheat berry (as nature grew it) these elements exist in perfect balance and further-

---

Gayelord Hauser, in his book Look Younger, Live Longer, *says, "No vitamin E and only two of the sixteen or more known B vitamins are added to devitalized bread ironically publicized as 'enriched.' What strange mathematics—to take away sixteen and add only two, and call the result 'enriched.' Such misbranding should be dealt with under the Pure Food and Drug Act."*

more create a rich nutty flavor which anyone can discover by chewing a few fresh, unground berries of wheat. The "enrichment" of bread consists of putting back into the defunct white flour one or two synthetic vitamins. The *other* vitamins and minerals and nature's balance, as well as the flavor of the original product are omitted. What we really have in these synthetically enriched products is something approaching a patent medicine lost in a welter of starch, and starch, of course is destitute of flavor. The white bread eater walks out of a grocery store with several loaves of white bread under his arm and in order to obtain any discernible nourishment, he must walk across the street to the drugstore and buy several bottles of vitamin pills. But even then he is missing a great deal in actual nourishment and downright eating pleasure. Also, sadly enough, diseases increase and fertility decreases.

Recent medical discoveries reported in *Time* magazine only recently show that vitamin E (which is present in the original wheat berry) benefits many types of heart disease. Reputable physicians after a great deal of research have discovered that the known increase in heart diseases may well be due to the over-refinement of foods such as the removal of the germ, and therefore of the vitamins and minerals from flour.

And when it comes to fertility, it is well established now that the oil in the germ is rich in vitamin E which confers upon mankind fertility and vigor.*

This germ is removed by modern milling processes.

VI

It might seem that I have wandered far from cooking. But this volume is an attempt, by the empirical method, to prove that everything good may still be made of *wholegrain* flour in spite of the fact that the millions of cook books in print today are based upon germless white flour. The impression has got about (and not un-

---

*We have received many letters from people who have benefitted by eating our wholegrain products. The one that pleased me the most was from a lovely girl I know who, after being married for five years without issue, began eating wholegrain at least twice a day, sometimes three. Ten months later I got a letter from her announcing the birth of two bouncing baby boys. Twins!

Of course we can't guarantee this every time.

aided) that you can cook nothing fit for human consumption of wholegrain products and that you need white flour to make beautiful light, fluffy bread, rolls, cakes, etc.

I sometimes wonder just how this food lightness and food whiteness got started. My hunch is that the lighter and whiter a food is, the less tasty and satisfying. I suspect that the desirability of making foods as light as a feather and as white as chalk was brought about, shrewdly, *after* the millers and bakers found by the removal of the germ, and by the introduction of bleaches and chemicals they could make food that, like any other embalmed thing, *kept* until it was sold! They have been able to educate the public into believing that lightness and whiteness are more important than taste and nutrition.

I strongly suspect that modern cooking, promoted by the cook books and cooking schools subsidized by manufacturers of refined and processed products, is a way of making something to eat that will quickly and completely fool the eater into thinking it is something good to eat. One has only to look at the brilliant display of items on the shelves of commercial bakers to realize that the eye-appeal is the main desideratum. I feel that many of us, until we are shown better, are very much like the woman who rushed home from a meeting of the Woman's Sewing Circle and, surrounded by her husband and children, exclaimed with great pride: "Oh, I learned a wonderful recipe for cake today from Mrs. Jones. She gave me her rule for making cake without using *any eggs or butter at all!*" The next step would be cheating at solitaire!

For thousands of years bread was made of genuine *wholegrain* flour, and man thrived. As a matter of fact the highest level of cooking as an art, as well as a method of fortifying the human frame, was reached in the 18th Century. Those great chefs of France, such as Brillat-Savarin and Monsieur Careme now considered the greatest cooks of all time, were plying their art before modern white patent flour was ever dreamt of. They cooked everything with *wholegrain* flour and firmly established cooking among the great arts of civilization. This was a contributing factor in making France one of the great civilized nations of the world.

"COOKING WITH WHOLEGRAINS" is not, however, a book for professional chefs or for those who believe that they can duplicate the

success of Brillat-Savarin and Careme. It is for everyday house-
wives and also men who are occasionally found in the kitchen, who
wish to cook something not only good to eat but good for them!

I will state unequivocally and without fear of contravention that
all edibles possible to be made of wheat, corn, oats, or rye, can be
cooked and better cooked with *wholegrain* wheat, corn, oats, and
rye, and what is more, better eaten and better for us.

The Vermont Guild of Oldtime Crafts and Industries here in
Weston was started in 1936 as a museum of early American crafts
and industries, and about twelve years ago began turning its stone
mill. Since that time thousands of people have cooked with these
wholegrains, but with the exception of a small brochure we issued
in 1938, there has not been available a comprehensive cooking book
dealing with more than a few recipes for wholegrain dishes.

VII

This volume which I am introducing is published because of the
increasing interest in wholegrains throughout the world, an interest
now being intensified by Gayelord Hauser's books on food and
good health.

Of a necessity, a quite different set of recipes is needed for *wholegrain* cooking than for cooking with germless commercial meals
and flour. In using wholegrain products, the relationship between
dry and liquid ingredients is different, and other ingredients change
in amounts, and especially the knack of combining them. For ex-
ample, wholegrain corn and wheat contain considerable natural
sweetness, and therefore it is never necessary strongly to fortify
them with sugar, as must be done when cooking with tasteless and
lifeless commercial flour.

It occurred to me that my wife probably knew as much about
cooking with wholegrains as any other woman not because of her
particular genius as a cook (although she is an excellent one), but
because in all these years we have been operating the stone mill
here in Vermont I have given her nothing to cook with *but* wholegrain products! Perforce, she has cooked with them. And over the
years from experience she has learned to cook well. Not only have
I lived and thrived but our two boys (now seven and nine in age)

have more energy than I ever thought possible to cram into so small a space.

Being a fellow who believes that things must work to be good, I was forced to the realization that my wife was the only person to prepare this cooking book. So this year she has been hard at work. Every recipe in this book has been cooked, not clipped. Every recipe in this book has been eaten, not sold. Many recipes in this book have been tried time and time again until the right blend was achieved.

I am proud to see that my wife has not committed the cardinal sin of some cooks I have seen and tussled with, and I refer to the sin of using any sugar at all in Southern, or Rhode Island johnny-cake, hoe cake or whatever you prefer to call it. Having eaten and drunk my way pleasantly from New Orleans to Philadelphia, I take off my hat to those lovely ladies of the South, who know by nature that wholegrain corn meal tickles the palate with its own natural sweetness, and that it is as sacrilegious to add sugar to corn dishes as it would be to erect a statue of Sherman in Atlanta.

Further, while those charming ladies of the Providence Plantations still swear by *white* corn meal, which I claim exhibits less than half the flavor and natural sweetness of yellow, I am ready to forgive this fall from grace on the ground that in my early days in their nation I relished with no little gusto the classic Rhode Island johnnycake, flavored with bacon fat, covered with South county butter, and washed down with a beer that was, the last I heard, still made in those parts, and a credit to the country.

My wife won't admit it, but I am of course somewhat of a cook myself! I sneak into the kitchen, particularly in the morning, and knock off muffins or pancakes, at will. However, if I were to write the recipes in this book, they would go something like the one for flapjacks I made last Sunday morning. I give you my recipe for what it may be worth:—

My Flapjacks

Dump some Irish or Scotch oatmeal into a large dish and into that some wholegrain wheat flour. Mix these together with the hands so that lumps are broken up. Then shake some baking powder out of the can into the mixture, and some salt. Mix again. In another dish beat up

*two eggs thoroughly until they run over the edge of the bowl. Pour this
liquid into the dry mixture and then add some milk and stir but not
beat. Melt some lard and when cool stir it in. Now you have some
flapjacks that when properly and slowly fried on a soapstone griddle
on top of a woodburning stove, and then dished onto a plate and covered
with butter and maple syrup are fit to eat.*

I suppose, however, that it would be difficult for some people to
follow such a recipe but frankly I cook by ear. I can never remember how much of anything. If you wish to cook this way, I suggest
that you eat a little raw wholegrain meal of different kinds and see
how it tastes. And since you know how milk, eggs and other ingredients taste you should be able to put them together in such a
way that when they get through everything tastes good. This is
my method of cooking.

Probably most women will be glad that this is not my wife's.

VIII

I want to say a word about bread which my wife has really paid
a great deal of attention to in the following recipes. It should be
obvious that the bakers' bread we eat nowadays is no longer the
staff of life. The most classic evidence of this was reported some
years ago in the British Medical Journal. It seems that Sir William
Wilcox discovered that in the hospitals of Egypt during the first
World War there existed an epidemic of beri-beri which knocked
off the white troops but not the Indians. When Sir William looked
into the matter he found that the Indian troops had been fed their
native flour made of wholewheat ground on stones. The white
troops had been treated a little better and fed white flour!

It is too bad that modern penology does not recognize the wis-
dom of punishments meted out to bread adulterators in the early
days. Records show that the making of bread has always been
regulated from the Middle Ages and that in the 18th Century it
was usual, when bread prices were raised too high, to hang a baker
or two. An authority writing of the bakers of Constantinople re-
lates that it was the custom of master bakers to keep a second
employee in reserve who in consideration of a small increase in his

weekly wage, agreed to appear before the court in case a victim was wanted. In Egypt bakers who sold adulterated bread were nailed to the door posts of their establishments by their ears.

I suppose it is too much to hope that this tradition will be slavishly followed by our government, and as a matter of cold fact, if most of the world wishes to eat sawdust, I don't know as it is any concern of mine. I shall have to be content in the hope that a chosen few who have been introduced to the wholesome, rich, nutty flavor of wholegrains will be now eager to try a hand at new and different ways of cooking with them.

IX

I would, however, make a final plea for the healthy exercise of the imagination. Cooking, being an art, is no different, at bottom, from any other art. The rules of painting, or the notes of an immortal sonata can be set carefully down, and in fact beautifully printed, but the result is still in the hands, mind, and heart of the practitioner. So with cooking.

The recipes that follow are, like the rules for mixing paints, or the symbols for finding notes on the keyboard, merely to guide you. They are basic recipes, and can, by minor changes, be varied in dozens of different ways. It is your imagination, and your technique (which may be no more than "just getting the right knack") that can help you reach the Olympian heights of all those who practice the culinary arts, where it is realized that we live to eat, rather than eat to live.

Vrest Orton

Bread & Rolls

THE BEST RECIPES in the world will not make a good bread-maker. There is a knack in making good bread, which like many other things in life, comes to one by doing after no little trial and error.

Cooking is not and never will be an exact science, nor indeed a science at all, except as it is practiced by commercial bakers who are able to manufacture, day in and day out, a standard product . . . nearly worthless as food, of course, but always durable, pretty to look at, and profitable.

Making good bread is an art! Besides dealing with live factors like the germ-content wholegrain flours, butter, eggs, fresh milk and so on, you are also dealing with temperature and humidity, and last but not least yourself. Bringing all these together, precisely in the same way, upon each occasion, time and time again, cannot be done and in fact ought not to be done.

If it were possible, and you could do so, cooking would lose the abiding pleasure that now lurks in it, and you would become sick and tired of the whole thing.

This is not a sermon, but only a warning. After you have followed a recipe for bread religiously, and it doesn't "come out" right, don't despair or suspect that the recipes are wrong. Try again.

And then, some bright Tuesday morning, you will enter the kitchen, take out this book, put some things together, and bake a bread that is so wonderful you wonder how it ever happened.

Once you do this, you will have the knack. Like learning to ride a bicycle, you can keep it with you as long as you like.

It's all in the point of view. Don't make cooking a science. Adopt it as an art. And be sure you consider another ingredient that is not mentioned anywhere in this book . . . and make use of it often. I refer to your wits.

V. O.

Wholewheat Bread

2 CUPS MILK, SCALDED	2 TEASPOONS SALT
3 TABLESPOONS HONEY	I YEAST CAKE
3 TABLESPOONS BUTTER	¼ CUP LUKEWARM WATER

WHEAT FLOUR (ABOUT 5 ½ CUPS)

This recipe is the result of years of trial and error, and I think provides almost a fool-proof way of making a good, comparatively light bread of wholegrain flour without any white flour at all. I emphasize here the vital necessity of punching down the dough, as described below, as this punch-bag technique is what takes the place of a lot of kneading and is what, really, distinguishes the method of making our genuine wholegrain bread from the methods employed by commercial bakers and those who bake with emaciated white flour.

Put the butter, honey and salt into a fairly large dish. Pour in the scalded milk and stir until the butter and honey are melted. Let cool until lukewarm, then add the yeast cake which has been dissolved in the ¼ cup of lukewarm water. Sift some wheat flour, then measure out 3 cups and sift into the liquid. Mix thoroughly, then add 2 more cups of wheat flour sifted the same way and mix as well. Now add more flour, a small amount at a time. Keep adding the wheat flour until the dough is so thick that you can no longer beat it with a spoon. It may require as much as 6 cups. When you think you have enough flour added, keep on mixing with the spoon for a minute or two longer, or as long as your arm will stand. Then cover closely and set in a warm place to rise.

The dough now needs to rise to about double in bulk. You then take a spoon, punch down the middle of the dough, fold the dough from the sides to the center until it is about turned over, and let the dough rise again. Do this *four* different times. Allow about an hour between risings, although the first one may take a little longer than the other three. Start the sponge the first thing in the morning and your bread will be finished in time to have hot rolls for supper.

You are now ready to turn the dough out on to a floured board or pastry cloth and you should be able to knead the bread without having it stick to the cloth or your hands any more than white bread does. You knead the whole batch for a minute or so until it seems firm. Then cut off two pounds of the dough, knead this for a minute or two, shape and put in the bread tin. Any remaining dough can be made into rolls or possibly two small loaves can be made from the whole batch. But 2 pounds of dough makes a nice fat, substantial looking loaf.

Let this rise in the tin until about double, then place in an oven pre-heated to 425°. This is *very important,* as the bread needs to start baking at this hot temperature to prevent falling. Let it bake at 425° for 15 minutes, then lower to 375° and bake 30 minutes longer . . . 45 minutes in all. If the bread has risen too much during the last rising it may fall a little, but the hot oven should prevent the bread from falling very much.

Salt-rising Bread

I CUP MILK
I TABLESPOON BROWN SUGAR

7 TABLESPOONS CORN MEAL
I TEASPOON SALT

Scald the milk and add the sugar, corn meal and salt. Put in a covered jar and place in a dish of water as hot as the hand can bear. Keep in a warm place overnight. By morning the mixture should show fermentation and gas can be heard to escape. Then add

2 CUPS SIFTED WHEAT FLOUR | 2 TABLESPOONS BROWN SUGAR
2 CUPS LUKEWARM WATER | 3 TABLESPOONS MELTED SHORTEN-
ING

Beat this mixture thoroughly, place in a dish of warm water again and let rise until light and full of bubbles. Then add about 4½ cups of sifted wheat flour, or enough to make a stiff dough. Knead for ten or fifteen minutes, then mold into loaves. Place in greased pans and let rise again until light.

Bake 15 minutes at 425°, then lower the temperature to 375° and bake about 30 minutes longer.

Rye Bread

2 CUPS MILK SCALDED | 1 YEAST CAKE DISSOLVED IN ¼ CUP
1 TABLESPOON SHORTENING | LUKEWARM WATER
2 TEASPOONS SALT | 4½ CUPS RYE

Scald the milk with the shortening. Add salt and when lukewarm add the dissolved yeast.

Sift the rye, measure and sift into the liquid. You should add enough rye to make a stiff but sticky dough. It should be moist enough to stir with a spoon. Continue stirring for 4 or 5 minutes the way you do when folding beaten egg whites into any mixture.

Cover closely and set in a warm place to rise until light (about 2 hours). Punch down and turn onto a board lightly sprinkled with rye. Knead for about 10 minutes, or until the dough begins to feel springy. Mold into loaves, cover, set in a warm place and let rise to about double. Bake 300° for 1½ hours with a pan of hot water placed in the oven underneath the bread.

Colonial Cottage Loaf

1 CUP MILK SCALDED | 1 YEAST CAKE
1 CUP HOT WATER | ¼ CUP LUKEWARM WATER
3 TABLESPOONS SHORTENING | 1¾ CUPS CORN MEAL
2 TABLESPOONS MOLASSES | 1¾ CUPS WHEAT FOUR
2 TEASPOONS SALT | 1¾ CUPS RYE

Pour the scalded milk and hot water over the shortening, mo-lasses and salt and stir until the shortening is dissolved. When lukewarm add the yeast cake dissolved in the quarter cup of lukewarm water. Sift the corn meal, wheat flour and rye separately, then measure and sift all together into the liquid. Stir with a spoon. The dough should be just soft enough to beat with a spoon.

Beat this mixture for 3 to 5 minutes or until you get tired of doing it longer. Then set in a warm place to rise for about 2 hours. When light and about double in bulk, beat it down again. Do this four different times as in the Wholewheat Bread recipe. Turn onto a board lightly sprinkled with wheat flour or some of the mixed flours. Knead until light (about 5 minutes) then shape into a round loaf and place in a 1 quart greased casserole. Let rise again until about double.

Bake for about 45 minutes, starting at 425° and lowering to 375° after 15 minutes. This makes a delicious, nutty flavored bread.

Pumpernickle

Pumpernickle is rye bread made with sour dough. Sour dough is dough saved over from a previous baking, preferably from the sponge stage before salt was added. Any dough that is not punched down or used when it has risen the full amount but is allowed to fall, is a sour dough. One-half to one cup of dough may be saved out from the sponge stage to use as a starter for the next baking, or to make a sour dough start with

½ YEAST CAKE DISSOLVED IN
2 CUPS LUKEWARM WATER. ADD
3 CUPS RYE, SIFTED BEFORE MEASURING AND AFTER

Mix well, then beat with a spoon for 2 minutes. Cover and set in a warm place to rise and fall. This sponge may be mixed up at night and allowed to rise overnight.

In the morning beat up the dough again, and add

1 TEASPOON SALT
1 CUP RYE
1 CUP SIFTED WHEAT FLOUR

Beat with a spoon for 3 minutes, cover and let rise again until light and spongy.

Punch down, turn onto a board covered with a mixture of half wheat flour and half rye and knead for about 10 minutes adding more of the mixed flour as required to keep the dough from sticking to the board. It may be necessary to work in one cup or more of the flour. When light and elastic in feeling, shape into a round loaf, place in a greased one quart glass casserole. Cover with a damp cloth and let rise until light and the surface starts to crack.

Bake at 300° for 1½ hours with a pan of hot water placed in the oven underneath the bread.

Rye and Wheat Bread

3 CUPS LUKEWARM WATER	5 TEASPOONS SALT
2 CAKES YEAST	5 CUPS RYE
3 TABLESPOONS BROWN SUGAR*	3 CUPS WHEAT FLOUR
3 TABLESPOONS MELTED SHORTENING	

Dissolve yeast in water. Add brown sugar, shortening and salt.

Sift the wheat flour and measure. Stir the rye and measure, then sift the wheat and rye all together and add about ¾ of this mixture to the liquid. Mix thoroughly, then add another cup of the flour, or enough more to make the dough stiff enough to knead.

Cover with a damp cloth, set in a warm place and let it rise until light. Punch down and let rise four different times as in whole wheat Bread Recipe. Then empty onto board and knead for a few minutes. Divide into two equal parts and knead and mold into loaves. Place in greased pans, cover with a damp cloth and let rise until light (nearly double in bulk) and bake 1½ hours at 300° with a pan of hot water in the oven underneath the bread.

Oatmeal Bread

2 CUPS WHEAT FLOUR	2½ TEASPOONS SALT
2 CUPS OATMEAL FLOUR	4 TABLESPOONS BROWN SUGAR
1½ CUPS MILK	2 TABLESPOONS SHORTENING
1 YEAST CAKE	(MELTED)
¼ CUP LUKEWARM WATER	HALF BUTTER AND HALF LARD

To make one loaf, pour scalded milk over Scotch oatmeal and mix well. Add yeast cake dissolved in lukewarm water, then salt, brown sugar and melted shortening (half butter, half lard).

Molasses can be substituted for brown sugar in this and other recipes.

Sift the wheat flour, measure, and add to the batter. Mix until all the flour is dampened, then beat with a spoon for 2 minutes. The dough should be thick enough so it is just possible to beat with a spoon.

Cover with a damp cloth, set in a warm place and let rise until light and soft when touched with the finger.

Punch down, cover with a damp cloth and let rise again. Then punch down again before turning out on a board sifted over with wheat flour. Knead 5 or 10 minutes. By this time the dough should not stick to the board at all.

Form into a loaf and place in a greased pan. Cover with a damp cloth, let rise to about double and bake 1 to 1½ hours at 300° with a pan of hot water placed in the oven underneath the bread.

Buttermilk Rolls

1 CUP BUTTERMILK, WARMED
3 TABLESPOONS SHORTENING
   (BUTTER AND LARD)
1 TEASPOON BROWN SUGAR
¼ TEASPOON SODA

1 YEAST CAKE
2¼ CUPS WHEAT FLOUR
1 TEASPOON BAKING POWDER
1¼ TEASPOONS SALT

Dissolve yeast cake in the warm buttermilk then add the melted shortening, brown sugar and soda and mix well. Sift the wheat flour, measure, add baking powder and salt and sift into the liquid all at once. Mix until the flour is all dampened then beat with a spoon for one minute. Cover with a damp cloth, set in a warm place and let rise to about double in bulk.

Punch down, let rise once more and turn onto a board covered with sifted wheat flour and knead until light and spongy (between 5 and 10 minutes). Mold into any desired size or shape, cover with a damp cloth again and let rise until light. Bake 15 to 20 minutes at 425°.

Wheat Rolls

2 CUPS SCALDED MILK
4 TABLESPOONS BUTTER OR SHORT-
   ENING
2 TABLESPOONS BROWN SUGAR OR
   HONEY
2½ TEASPOONS SALT

1 YEAST CAKE
¼ CUP LUKEWARM WATER
2 EGGS WELL BEATEN
5 CUPS WHEAT FLOUR (APPROXI-
   MATELY)

Scald milk with shortening, then pour over sweetening and salt. When lukewarm add the yeast dissolved in the lukewarm water and after that the well beaten eggs.

Sift the wheat flour, measure and sift into the liquid using about 4 cups to start with. Mix well and add enough more wheat flour to make a dough as stiff as you can have it but still be able to beat with a spoon for two minutes.

Cover closely and allow to rise in a warm place until almost double. Punch down and let rise again. The punching down process is important as it prevents stretching of the dough.

Knead until light and elastic. Mold into rolls of any desired shape. Cover with a damp cloth and let rise until light. Bake at 425° 15 to 20 minutes. This recipe makes 2 dozen rolls.

French Brioche

1 YEAST CAKE	¾ POUND BUTTER
¼ CUP LUKEWARM WATER	2 TEASPOONS SALT
4 CUPS WHEAT FLOUR	2 TABLESPOONS SUGAR
7 EGGS	

Dissolve the yeast cake in lukewarm water, then add enough wheat flour to make a very soft ball of paste. Drop this ball into a bowl of warm water (the water must not be hot or it will kill the yeast plant). Cover, and set in a warm place to rise. The ball of paste will sink to the bottom of the water at first, but will rise to the top later, and be full of bubbles.

Put the rest of the flour in a large bowl, make a hole in the center of it and into this hole put the softened butter, salt, sugar and 4 eggs. Break the eggs in whole. Work together with a spoon gradually working in the flour. Add 2 more eggs, one at a time, as you need more moisture. Beat this with a spoon for 5 minutes or so.

When the ball of paste has risen to become light and full of bubbles, lift it out of the water with a skimmer and mix into the dough, adding the last egg. Beat this mixture for a long time. The longer it is beaten, the better and finer will be the grain.

Put the dough in a bowl, cover and let rise to double its size. Beat it down again and place in the refrigerator for at least 12 hours. After removing from the refrigerator, handle the dough delicately and quickly as it softens as it becomes warm. This dough may be shaped into braided rolls, or buns of any desired shape, or tiny loaves of bread. If a glazed top is desired, brush over with egg yolk diluted with water before putting in the oven. Always serve hot or very fresh.

Bake at 425° about 20 minutes.

MUFFIN MEAL RECIPES

Muffin Meal, a mixture or amalgamation of wholegrain wheat, corn and rye fused together on the stone mill, provides a basic and simple grain product that can be used in hundreds of ways. A few typical examples are given below and your own ingenuity can provide many others.

Muffins

2 EGGS
I CUP MILK
6 TABLESPOONS MELTED SHORTEN-
    ING
I ½ CUPS MUFFIN MEAL

2 ½ TEASPOONS BAKING POWDER
2 TABLESPOONS BROWN SUGAR OR
    HONEY
¾ TEASPOON SALT

Beat the eggs. Add milk, sweetening and melted shortening. Sift the Muffin Meal, measure, add baking powder and salt. Sift this into the liquid and stir only enough to dampen the meal . . . do not beat. Let stand a minute or two while greasing the muffin pans. Drop mixture by spoonfuls into the muffin pans and bake at 425° for about 20 minutes.

Hot Bread

I ⅓ CUPS MUFFIN MEAL
I TEASPOON CREAM OF TARTAR
½ TEASPOON SODA
¾ TEASPOON SALT

I CUP MILK
4 TABLESPOONS SUGAR OR HONEY
4 TABLESPOONS SHORTENING,
    MELTED
I EGG BEATEN

Mix together the beaten egg, milk, sweetening and shortening. Sift the Muffin Meal, measure and add other dry ingredients. Sift into the liquid. Beat up quickly, pour into a greased square pan and bake at 425° for about 20 minutes.

Buttermilk Quick Bread

I ¾ CUPS MUFFIN MEAL	¾ TEASPOON SALT
I TEASPOON CREAM OF TARTAR	I CUP BUTTERMILK
½ TEASPOON SODA	2 EGGS WELL BEATEN
2 TABLESPOONS BROWN SUGAR OR HONEY	3 TABLESPOONS MELTED SHORTENING

Beat the eggs, and add buttermilk, melted shortening and sugar or honey. Sift the Muffin Meal, measure, add other dry ingredients, then sift into the liquid. Beat up quickly until free of lumps. Pour into a greased square pan and bake at 425° for about 20 minutes.

Molasses Quick Bread

I EGG BEATEN	½ TEASPOON SODA
½ CUP MOLASSES	I TEASPOON BAKING POWDER
I CUP BUTTERMILK	I TEASPOON SALT
¼ CUP MELTED SHORTENING	½ CUP SEEDLESS RAISINS
2 CUPS MUFFIN MEAL	

Beat the egg, add molasses, buttermilk and shortening and mix. Sift the Muffin Meal, measure, add soda, baking powder, and salt and sift into the liquid. Pour raisins on top of flour mixture and stir up quickly all at once until well mixed. Bake in a bread pan at 350° for 45 minutes.

Steamed Brown Bread

3 CUPS MUFFIN MEAL	2 CUPS SOUR MILK
2 TEASPOONS SODA	2 TABLESPOONS MELTED SHORTENING
I TEASPOON SALT	
⅔ CUP MOLASSES	½ CUP RAISINS

Mix together the sour milk and molasses. Sift the Muffin Meal, measure, add soda and salt, then sift into the liquid. Pour raisins on top of flour mixture and mix all together. Add shortening last.

Pour into a greased mold, having the mold no more than ⅔ full, cover closely. Place in a dish of hot water, having the water come half way up on the mold. Steam 3½ hours. If placed in several small molds, steam 2 hours.

Griddlecakes

2 EGGS, BEATEN	2 CUPS MUFFIN MEAL
1 ¼ CUPS MILK	3 TABLESPOONS SUGAR OR HONEY
¼ CUP MELTED SHORTENING	¾ TEASPOON SALT
	5 TEASPOONS BAKING POWDER

Beat eggs, add milk, sweetening and melted shortening, and mix well. Sift Muffin Meal, measure, add salt and baking powder. Sift into the liquid ingredients. Mix up very quickly, stirring only enough to dampen the meal. Cook slowly on moderately hot griddle until golden brown and serve with Vermont maple syrup, honey, or jam.

Jam Hot Cakes

2 or 3 tablespoons of jam or jelly used in the above recipe in place of the sugar or honey makes an interesting new kind of hot cake which can be eaten best with butter between the cakes piled at least three high, and maple syrup poured over all.

Buttermilk Griddlecakes

1 EGG, BEATEN	1 CUP MUFFIN MEAL
1 CUP BUTTERMILK	½ TEASPOON SODA
2 TABLESPOONS MAPLE SYRUP OR HONEY	1 TEASPOON BAKING POWDER
4 TABLESPOONS MELTED SHORTENING	¾ TEASPOON SALT

Beat the egg, add buttermilk, sweetening and shortening. Sift the Muffin Meal, measure, add soda, baking powder and salt and sift into the liquid. Mix up quickly, stirring only enough to dampen the meal. Cook on greased hot griddle until golden brown and serve with Vermont maple syrup or honey.

Quick Breads, Steamed Breads & Doughnuts

Countryman's Corn Bread

(With sour milk or buttermilk)

I CUP CORN MEAL
I CUP WHEAT FLOUR
I TEASPOON CREAM OF TARTAR
½ TEASPOON SODA
2 TABLESPOONS BROWN SUGAR

¾ TEASPOON SALT
I CUP SOUR MILK OR BUTTERMILK
2 EGGS WELL BEATEN
3 TABLESPOONS MELTED SHORTEN-
ING

Beat the eggs. Add sour milk or buttermilk. Sift the wheat flour, measure, add all other dry ingredients and sift into the liquid. Add melted shortening, mix all together and beat for a second or two.

Pour into a greased 8 x 8 inch pan, or a pan 1½ inches deep and bake about 20 minutes at 425°.

Corn Meal and Wheat Quick Bread

⅔ CUP CORN MEAL
⅔ CUP WHEAT FLOUR
I TEASPOON CREAM OF TARTAR
½ TEASPOON SODA
I CUP MILK

¾ TEASPOON SALT
4 TABLESPOONS BROWN SUGAR
4 TABLESPOONS SHORTENING
I EGG BEATEN

Cut the shortening into the combined dry ingredients with a pastry cutter. Add the egg and milk beaten together. Give a few quick beats with the spoon, pour into greased 8 x 8 inch pan and bake at 425° about 20 minutes.

Early American Hot Bread

⅔ CUP CORN MEAL
I EGG
I CUP MILK
2 TABLESPOONS MAPLE SYRUP OR HONEY

¾ CUP WHEAT FLOUR
2½ TEASPOONS BAKING POWDER
I TEASPOON SALT
3 TABLESPOONS MELTED SHORTEN-ING

Beat egg until light. Add milk and Vermont maple syrup. Mix together the dry ingredients, and sift into the liquid. Add melted shortening. Stir briskly and bake in 8 x 8 inch pan for 20 minutes at 425°. This hot bread is grand provender for growing kids to thrive on.

Southern Corn Bread

2 CUPS MILK
I CUP CORN MEAL
I TEASPOON SALT

2 TABLESPOONS BUTTER
2 EGGS, WELL BEATEN
I TEASPOON BAKING POWDER

Scald corn meal and milk together. Add the butter. Beat with an egg beater until smooth, cool slightly, and add eggs, baking powder and salt. Bake in greased 8 x 8 inch pan 20 to 25 minutes at 425°.

Sugar must never be used in Southern corn bread. The natural sweetness of the corn is sufficent.

Spoon Bread

1 CUP CORN MEAL	2 EGGS WELL BEATEN
1 ½ CUPS BOILING WATER	½ TEASPOON SALT
1 ½ CUPS MILK	½ TEASPOON BAKING POWDER

Stir corn meal into boiling water. Remove from fire and add the milk slowly, then eggs, salt and baking powder. Bake the mixture in a deep buttered pan or casserole for a half hour or longer at 425°. Don't be afraid to set this dish right on the table in the pan or casserole in which it is cooked. Serve smoking hot by the table-spoonful from the pan with a pat of butter tucked into its middle.

Suet Corn Bread

(*sour milk*)

1 EGG BEATEN	½ TEASPOON SODA
1 CUP SOUR MILK OR BUTTERMILK	¾ TEASPOON SALT
1 ¼ CUPS CORN MEAL	⅛ CUP CHOPPED SUET

Beat the egg and add the sour milk or buttermilk and mix well. Crush soda in the palm of hand to remove lumps and add it, with salt, to the corn meal and mix with a spoon. Add the chopped suet to this corn meal mixture and mix until crumbly, then combine the wet and dry ingredients. Mix well and bake at 425° for 20 minutes.

Quick Brown Bread

1 EGG BEATEN	½ TEASPOON SODA
½ CUP MOLASSES	1 TEASPOON BAKING POWDER
1 CUP SOUR MILK OR BUTTERMILK	1 TEASPOON SALT
¼ CUP MELTED SHORTENING	½ CUP SEEDLESS RAISINS
2 CUPS WHEAT FLOUR	

Beat the egg, add molasses, sour milk and shortening.

Sift the wheat flour, measure, add soda, baking powder and salt and sift into the liquid. Pour raisins on top and stir up quickly all at once. Bake in a bread pan at 350° for 45 minutes.

Quick Coffee Cake

1 ½ CUPS WHEAT FLOUR
½ TEASPOON SODA
1 TEASPOON CREAM OF TARTAR
¾ TEASPOON SALT

½ CUP BROWN SUGAR
¼ CUP SHORTENING
1 EGG BEATEN
½ CUP MILK

Topping: 2 TABLESPOONS MELTED BUTTER
4 TABLESPOONS BROWN SUGAR
1 TABLESPOON WHEAT FLOUR
CINNAMON

Sift the wheat flour, measure, add the other dry ingredients and sift again. Blend in the shortening, then add the egg and milk beaten together. Mix quickly with a spoon then beat slightly.

Spread in a round or square cake pan (the pan should be 1½ inches deep). Cover the top with the melted butter, then sprinkle on the brown sugar, wheat flour and cinnamon. Bake 20 minutes at 425°.

Yorkshire Pudding

2 EGGS BEATEN
1 CUP BUTTERMILK
1 CUP CORN MEAL

½ TEASPOON SODA
¼ TEASPOON SALT

Beat all together with an egg beater for two minutes. Remove meat from roaster, leaving some fat in bottom of the pan. Pour mixture into roaster and bake about 20 minutes at 425°. If the roaster is large it will be necessary to double the recipe.

This may also be baked in a square shallow cake pan with about 4 tablespoons of fat from the roast put in the bottom of the pan. Tip the pan so the fat will grease the sides too. However, we recommend using the roaster if possible as the drippings from the roast make this dish really toothsome.

Boston Brown Bread

½ CUP MOLASSES
2 TABLESPOONS MELTED SHORTEN-
    ING
1 ½ CUPS SOUR MILK OR BUTTER-
    MILK
1 CUP OATMEAL FLOUR

1 CUP WHEAT FLOUR
½ CUP CORN MEAL
¾ TEASPOON SALT
1 ½ TEASPOONS SODA
½ CUP RAISINS

Mix together the molasses, shortening and sour milk or butter-milk. Add the oatmeal. Sift the wheat flour, measure, add corn meal, salt and soda and sift into the batter. Add raisins and beat well.

Pour into a greased mold having the mold no more than ⅔ full. Cover closely. Place in a dish of hot water having the water come half way up on the mold. Steam 3 hours.

If placed in several small molds, steam 2 hours.

Vermont Brown Bread

(*with sour milk*)

1 CUP CORN MEAL
1 CUP SIFTED RYE
1 CUP WHEAT FLOUR
2 TEASPOONS SODA

1 TEASPOON SALT
⅔ CUP MOLASSES
2 CUPS SOUR MILK
2 TABLESPOONS MELTED SHORTEN-
    ING

Combine molasses and sour milk. Add dry ingredients well mixed together, then shortening. Mix well. Pour into well-greased mold ⅔ full. Cover closely and steam 3½ hours, having boiling water come up half way around mold. Half a cup of raisins may be added to the dry ingredients if your taste so dictates a richer dish.

And the Same

(*with sweet milk*)

We believe that the recipe above, using sour milk creates a concoction of superior merit, particularly for Saturday night with baked beans. We feel it is worthwhile souring the milk especially for this recipe. But, if you want to make it with sweet milk, here's how: Follow the above instructions except use 1½ cups sweet milk in place of the sour, and reduce soda to ½ teaspoon and add 2 teaspoons baking powder.

Doughnuts

2 EGGS BEATEN
1 CUP SUGAR
2 TABLESPOONS MELTED SHORTEN-
    ING
1 CUP SOUR MILK OR BUTTERMILK
4 CUPS WHEAT FLOUR

½ TEASPOON SODA
1 ½ TEASPOONS BAKING POWDER
1 ¼ TEASPOONS SALT
1 TEASPOON NUTMEG
½ TEASPOON CINNAMON

Add sugar and shortening to beaten eggs, then the sour milk or buttermilk and beat.

Sift wheat flour, measure, add soda, baking powder, salt, nutmeg and cinnamon and sift into the liquid. Mix thoroughly.

Turn out on a board covered with wheat flour. Knead for a half minute, then pat or roll out to ⅜ inch thickness. Cut out with doughnut cutter and fry in deep hot fat.

Buckwheat Hot Bread

1 EGG BEATEN
3 TABLESPOONS MOLASSES
¼ CUP SOUR CREAM
¾ CUP BUTTERMILK

1 CUP BUCKWHEAT FLOUR
½ CUP WHEAT FLOUR
½ TEASPOON SODA
1 TEASPOON CREAM OF TARTAR
½ TEASPOON SALT

Beat egg, add molasses, sour cream and buttermilk. Sift buckwheat and wheat flours, measure, add soda, cream of tartar and salt and sift all into the liquid. Beat up quickly and bake in an 8 x 8 x 2 in. pan at 350° for 20 minutes. This will burn if the oven is too hot.

Muffins, Popovers & Gems

The secret of good light muffins is to avoid overmixing, to sift dry ingredients together once and quickly, and to dash the mixture into muffin pans with speed and dispatch and without yielding to the temptation to beat. Tender, fine texture muffins will result if recipe is followed faithfully.

Wheat Muffins

1⅔ CUPS WHEAT FLOUR
2¼ TEASPOONS BAKING POWDER
3 TABLESPOONS BROWN SUGAR
1 TEASPOON SALT

1 EGG BEATEN
1⅓ CUPS SWEET MILK
4 TABLESPOONS MELTED SHORTEN-
ING

Mix together the wheat flour, brown sugar, baking powder and salt. Beat egg until light, add milk and slightly cooled shortening. Toss in the wheat flour mixture and stir quickly just enough to dampen the flour. Let stand a few minutes until mixture thickens then drop by spoonfuls into muffin tins and bake (425°) 20 to 25 minutes. Raisins or nuts may be added to the mixture or sprinkled on top of muffins before placing in oven. A small spoonful of jam or jelly may also be placed on each muffin.

Corn Meal and Wheat Muffins

1 CUP CORN MEAL
¾ CUP WHEAT FLOUR
2 TEASPOONS BAKING POWDER
2 TEASPOONS BROWN SUGAR

¾ TEASPOON SALT
2 EGGS, WELL BEATEN
1 CUP MILK
4 TABLESPOONS MELTED SHORTEN-
ING

Sift wheat flour once, measure and add the baking powder, salt and sugar . . . now add corn meal and sift once more and mix well. Combine the milk, eggs and shortening and add to dry ingredients stirring only to dampen mixture. Bake in greased pans in hot oven (425°) about 25 minutes or until done. You can make corn bread-sticks by using bread-stick pans. Try splitting the leftover muffins and toasting them, for a morning meal.

Corn Meal and Rye Muffins

1 CUP CORN MEAL
1 CUP RYE
2 ¼ TEASPOONS BAKING POWDER
2 TEASPOONS HONEY

¾ TEASPOON SALT
2 EGGS, WELL BEATEN
1 CUP MILK
4 TABLESPOONS MELTED SHORTEN-
ING

Sift together the dry ingredients. Combine the milk, eggs, slightly cooled shortening and honey. Add to dry ingredients stirring only enough to dampen. Spoon mixture into muffin pans and bake at 425° 20 or 25 minutes or until done. Makes 12 muffins. (Delicious served with honey.)

Rye and Wheat Muffins

1 CUP RYE

1 TEASPOON SALT

¾ CUP WHEAT FLOUR

1 TEASPOON CREAM OF TARTAR

½ TEASPOON SODA

2 TABLESPOONS BROWN SUGAR

2 EGGS, WELL BEATEN

1 CUP MILK

¼ CUP SHORTENING, MELTED

Beat eggs, add milk and shortening. Then add dry ingredients in order given. Mix all together quickly, but do not beat. Bake in muffin tins at 425° about 20 minutes.

Combination Muffins

½ CUP CORN MEAL

1 TABLESPOON SUGAR

1 TEASPOON SALT

1 TABLESPOON BUTTER

2½ CUPS BOILING WATER

½ CUP EACH CORN, RYE AND WHEAT FLOURS

2 TEASPOONS BAKING POWDER

1 EGG, WELL BEATEN

Cook ½ cup corn meal, sugar, salt, butter and boiling water in top of double boiler one hour. Remove from fire and when cool add balance of corn meal, rye and wheat mixed with baking powder. Fold in beaten egg and bake in iron gem pans or muffin cups for 20 minutes in hot oven, 425°.

Blueberry Muffins

Add ½ to 1 cup of blueberries to corn meal and wheat muffins. Increase sugar to 4 tablespoons.

Nut Muffins

Add ½ cup of chopped nuts to corn meal and wheat muffins or muffins containing rye.

Raisin Muffins

Add ½ cup of raisins to corn meal and wheat muffins or muffins with rye, or place raisins on top of muffins before baking.

Jam Muffins

Before baking corn meal and wheat muffins or muffins with rye in them, place ½ teaspoon of jam, jelly or marmalade on top of each muffin.

Corn Gems

2 EGGS, SEPARATED
1 CUP BUTTERMILK
3 TABLESPOONS SHORTENING
½ CUP BUCKWHEAT OR WHEAT
    FLOUR OR RYE

1 CUP CORN MEAL
½ TEASPOON SODA
1 TEASPOON BAKING POWDER
1 TEASPOON SALT

Beat the egg yolks with a spoon. Add buttermilk and shortening and stir again. Sift the buckwheat, wheat or rye, measure, add corn meal, soda, baking powder and salt and sift into the liquid. Stir as little as possible to dampen the flour. Fold in beaten egg whites and pour into warm gem pans. Bake at 425° about 20 minutes.

Kernel Corn Cakes

¾ CUP CORN MEAL
2 TEASPOONS BAKING POWDER
1½ TEASPOONS SUGAR
½ TEASPOON SALT

2 EGGS WELL BEATEN
½ CUP MILK
1 CUP KERNEL CORN OR NIBLETS

Beat eggs until light. Add milk and corn. Mix together the dry ingredients and combine with liquid mixture. Bake in muffin pans in moderately hot oven 425° for about 20 minutes, and you'll have a dish that gives you that luscious natural corn flavor.

Oatmeal Muffins

1 CUP HOT BUTTERMILK
1 CUP FLOUR OATMEAL
1 EGG BEATEN
3 TABLESPOONS BROWN SUGAR
¼ CUP MELTED SHORTENING

1 CUP WHEAT FLOUR
½ TEASPOON SODA
1 TEASPOON BAKING POWDER
1 TEASPOON SALT

Pour the hot buttermilk over the oatmeal, mix, and let it stand while beating the egg. When the oatmeal is thick and slightly cooled add the egg, sugar and shortening, then beat with a spoon for one minute. Sift the wheat flour, measure, add baking powder, soda and salt and sift into the batter. The important thing now is to mix only enough to dampen the wheat. Let the mixture stand in the bowl while greasing the muffin pans. The mixture will start to rise or puff up. Do not disturb this lightness as you gently and carefully fill the tins. Put a heaping mixing spoonful into each muffin cup, until you have one dozen muffins.

Bake in a hot oven 425° about 20 minutes. These muffins should come out light and crisp with a real oatmeal flavor.

Corn Meal Popovers

1 ¼ CUPS CORN MEAL	3 EGGS
2 CUPS MILK	¾ TEASPOON SALT
1 TABLESPOON BUTTER	

Scald the corn meal with the milk, add butter and salt and beat thoroughly. When cool add the well beaten eggs, beat two minutes with a spoon and pour into hot iron gem pans or muffin cups. Bake 20 to 25 minutes in a hot oven 450°. These are really delicious.

Rye or Wheat Popovers

2 EGGS, WELL BEATEN	1 CUP RYE, OR WHEAT FLOUR OR A
1 CUP MILK	COMBINATION OF BOTH
1 TABLESPOON SHORTENING	½ TEASPOON SALT

Mix beaten eggs, milk and shortening. Sift the rye or wheat, measure, add salt and sift into the liquid. Beat with an egg beater for 2 minutes. Bake for 10 minutes at 500° then decrease to 350° and bake 20 minutes longer.

Popovers lend themselves well to wholegrain flours because they are made without sugar or leavening agents and the finished product reveals the natural, true flavor of the wholegrain. Popovers are raised by steam instead of baking powder or soda. Therefore, it is imperative that they go into a very hot oven (500°) in order that a crust be formed immediately. As soon as they begin to brown the temperature is gradually lowered to 350° to finish the baking.

Biscuits, Griddlecakes, Scones & Dumplings

Baking Powder Biscuits

2 CUPS WHEAT OR RYE FLOUR
1 TEASPOON SALT
3 TEASPOONS BAKING POWDER

4 TABLESPOONS SHORTENING
1 CUP MILK (APPROXIMATELY)

Sift wheat or rye flour, measure, add salt and baking powder and sift again. Blend in shortening, then add enough milk to make a moist dough.

Turn onto a wheat floured board, pat or roll out to ½ inch thickness, cut out biscuits and bake at 475° for about 15 minutes.

Sour Cream Biscuits

2 CUPS WHEAT FLOUR
1 TEASPOON SODA
1 TEASPOON SALT

¾ CUP SOUR CREAM
¼ CUP SWEET MILK

Sift wheat flour, measure, add soda and salt and sift again. Add sour cream and milk to make a moist biscuit dough. A little more milk may be needed. Beat for a minute with a spoon, then roll out ½ inch thick if you wish and cut out with a biscuit cutter, or shape into biscuits with the hands or a spoon.

Bake at 475° 12 to 15 minutes. If you like fat biscuits, place close together in a pan 8 inches square. If you like crisp biscuits, place 1 inch apart on a cookie sheet.

Rye Biscuits

2½ CUPS RYE
1 TEASPOON SALT
½ TEASPOON SODA

1 TEASPOON CREAM OF TARTAR
3 TABLESPOONS BUTTER
1 CUP MILK

Sift the rye, measure, add salt, cream of tartar and soda and sift again. Blend in butter then add enough milk (about 1 cup) to make a moist dough and beat briskly for a minute.

Empty out on a wheat floured board, pat down, turn over and roll out ½ inch thick. Do not knead. Cut into biscuit shape and bake at 475° 12 to 15 minutes.

If you like crisp biscuits, place one inch apart on a cookie sheet. If you like them soft, place close together in a pan 8 inches square.

Cream Scones

2 CUPS WHEAT FLOUR
2 TEASPOONS BAKING POWDER
½ TEASPOON SALT
2 TEASPOONS BROWN SUGAR

4 TABLESPOONS BUTTER
2 EGGS, BEATEN
⅓ CUP LIGHT CREAM

Sift the wheat flour, measure, add baking powder, salt and sugar and sift into bowl. Blend in butter.

Save out a small portion of egg white and beat remainder of eggs. Add to the flour mixture with the cream. Stir up quickly and beat with a spoon for a minute. Turn out on wheat floured board, roll out ½ inch thick and cut in any desired shape. Place on cookie sheet, brush tops with egg white, slightly beaten, and sprinkle with brown sugar.

Bake at 450° 12 to 15 minutes.

Dumplings

2 CUPS WHEAT FLOUR	¾ TEASPOON SALT
4 TEASPOONS BAKING POWDER	⅛ CUP MILK (APPROXIMATELY)

Sift wheat flour, measure, add baking powder and salt and sift again. Add milk enough to make a sticky dough. Drop by spoonfuls on top of stew, and steam 12 minutes without lifting the cover.

Corn Meal Dumplings

Follow recipe for Corn Dodgers, see page 45. Drop by spoonfuls on top of stew or greens and steam about 20 minutes.

Wheat Griddle Cakes

2 CUPS WHEAT FLOUR	2 EGGS, BEATEN
2 TABLESPOONS BROWN SUGAR	1 ½ CUPS SWEET MILK
3 TEASPOONS BAKING POWDER	5 TABLESPOONS MELTED SHORTEN-
1 TEASPOON SALT	ING

Mix together the wheat flour, baking powder and salt. Beat eggs until light, add milk, brown sugar and shortening. Quickly toss in the dry ingredients and stir only enough to dampen the flour. Brown on hot griddle and serve at once with Vermont maple syrup, honey, or applesauce.

Buttermilk Griddlecakes

I EGG, BEATEN
I CUP BUTTERMILK
2 TABLESPOONS MAPLE SYRUP OR
   HONEY
4 TABLESPOONS MELTED SHORTEN-
   ING

⅓ CUP CORN MEAL, AND ⅔ CUP
   WHEAT FLOUR (OR I CUP OF
   ANY WHOLE GRAIN)
½ TEASPOON SODA
I TEASPOON BAKING POWDER
¾ TEASPOON SALT

Beat the egg, add buttermilk, sweetening and shortening. Sift wheat meal, measure, add corn meal, soda, baking powder and salt and sift into liquid. Mix up quickly stirring only enough to dampen the flour. Bake on greased hot griddle.

Corn Meal and Wheat Griddlecakes

⅓ CUP CORN MEAL
⅔ CUP WHEAT MEAL
I TEASPOON CREAM OF TARTAR
½ TEASPOON SODA
¾ TEASPOON SALT

3 TABLESPOONS BROWN SUGAR
3 TABLESPOONS SHORTENING
I EGG
¾ CUP MILK

Cut the shortening into the combined dry ingredients with a pastry cutter. Add the egg and milk beaten together. Cook on moderately hot greased griddle. If the griddle is too hot the cakes will burn and not cook through properly.

Serve with maple syrup or honey or applesauce.

Quick Buckwheat Cakes

I CUP BUCKWHEAT
½ TEASPOON SODA
¾ TEASPOON SALT

½ CUP SOUR CREAM
I CUP MILK, APPROXIMATELY

Mix buckwheat, soda and salt, then add sour cream and enough milk to make a thin batter.

Then remember the rule for buckwheat cakes. A *hot*, well-greased griddle for frying.

Raised Buckwheat Cakes

1 CUP BUCKWHEAT	3/4 TEASPOON SALT
1/2 CUP CORN MEAL	2 CUPS BOILING WATER
1/2 CUP WHEAT FLOUR	1/2 YEAST CAKE
1/2 CUP MILK	1/4 TEASPOON SODA

Scald the corn meal and salt with the boiling water. Beat well and when cool add the buckwheat and wheat flours, then dissolved yeast. Let stand overnight, covered. In the morning add the soda dissolved in milk. Cook on hot, well-greased griddle in small cakes quickly.

Save a cup of batter to serve as a starter for the next day.

The two following recipes for buckwheat cakes, sweetened with maple sugar, are old ones which have been used in a Vermont family for several generations.

Maple Sugar Buckwheat Cakes No. 1

1 CUP THICK SOUR CREAM	1 TEASPOON SODA
1 EGG, BEATEN	1/2 TEASPOON BAKING POWDER
1/2 CUP MAPLE SUGAR	1 CUP BUCKWHEAT FLOUR
	1/4 TEASPOON SALT

Beat the egg, add sour cream and maple sugar and mix until the sugar is dissolved. Measure the buckwheat flour, add other dry ingredients and sift into liquid. Mix up quickly to a very thick mixture. Drop by spoonfuls on a greased griddle, leaving space between the cakes. As they cook they spread out. Serve with plenty of butter and maple syrup and you have something really delicious, if you like buckwheat.

Maple Sugar Buckwheat Cakes No. 2

1 CUP OF SOUR MILK	1/8 CUP WHEAT FLOUR
1/2 CUP MAPLE SUGAR	1/2 TEASPOON BAKING POWDER
1/4 CUP MELTED SHORTENING	1 TEASPOON SODA
1 CUP BUCKWHEAT FLOUR	PINCH OF SALT

Mix together the sour milk, maple sugar and shortening. Sift the dry ingredients into the liquid mixture and cook on a hot griddle until done. Serve with butter and maple syrup or honey.

Kentucky Raised Buckwheat Cakes

1 CUP CORN MEAL
2 CUPS BUCKWHEAT FLOUR
2 CUPS TEPID WATER
2 TABLESPOONS MELTED SHORTEN-
    ING
1 TEASPOON SALT

½ YEAST CAKE
4 TABLESPOONS MILK
½ TEASPOON SODA
2 TABLESPOONS MOLASSES

Dissolve yeast in 1 cup of the tepid water. Mix together the corn meal, sifted buckwheat flour and salt. Add the yeast, remainder of water and melted shortening, and beat well. Let rise overnight in warm kitchen. In the morning mix together the milk, soda and molasses. Add to the batter and let rise until ready to use. Then bake on hot griddle and serve with honey, Vermont maple syrup or, if you prefer southern style, you could use molasses or sorghum. It is important that the griddle be well greased.

Buckwheat-Rice Griddlecakes

1 CUP WARM BOILED RICE
1 CUP MILK
¾ TEASPOON SALT
2 EGG YOLKS

2 EGG WHITES
1 TABLESPOON MELTED BUTTER
¾ CUP BUCKWHEAT FLOUR
1 TEASPOON BAKING POWDER

Mix together milk, rice and salt. Add beaten egg yolks, butter, buckwheat and baking powder. Fold in beaten egg whites. Cook on hot, well-greased griddle.

Batter Cakes

2 CUPS CORN MEAL MUSH
½ CUP WHEAT FLOUR

¾ TEASPOON SALT
2 EGGS BEATEN
MILK

Add the beaten eggs to the corn meal mush, then the sifted wheat flour and salt. Mix in enough sweet milk to make a batter not too thick and not too thin. The amount required depends on the consistency of the mush.

Cook on a fairly hot greased griddle, browning both sides of the cakes. These take a little longer to cook than regular griddlecakes, so allow a little extra time. However, they are well worth waiting for.

Like pones, they may take the place of bread, or be eaten like griddlecakes for breakfast.

Corn Pone

I CUP CORN MEAL
¾ TEASPOON SALT
⅜ TEASPOON SODA

¾ CUP BUTTERMILK
I TABLESPOON FAT

Mix together the corn meal, salt and soda. Add buttermilk and mix well.

Melt the fat in a spider and drop the batter by spoonfuls into the spider. Cover and cook over low heat. When one side is brown, turn the cakes over, cover again and continue cooking. It should take about 30 minutes altogether.

These are delicious served with butter in place of bread with any meal, or with maple syrup or honey they make a nice breakfast or luncheon dish.

Corn Dodgers

2 CUPS CORN MEAL
4 TABLESPOONS SHORTENING

I TEASPOON SALT
COLD WATER

Blend shortening into corn meal and salt with fingertips or a pastry blender. Add enough cold water to moisten thoroughly having the mixture slightly more moist than piecrust.

Shape into round cakes ½ inch thick. Place on a well-greased griddle and cook slowly until brown and crusty. Turn and cook the other side the same. Serve with lots of butter and maple syrup or honey.

OR, place on a well-greased cookie sheet and bake in a moderate oven until done.

Pioneer's Hoe Cake

2 CUPS CORN MEAL   ABOUT 2 ½ CUPS BOILING WATER
I TEASPOON SALT

Mix together the corn meal, and salt and then pour over it the boiling water and mix thoroughly to form thick batter. Now grease a griddle with bacon fat and spread out batter into cakes about half-inch thick or a little less. Grease griddle between fryings, or put daub of butter atop each cake before turning. Cook until golden brown and serve hot with butter and Vermont maple syrup or honey.

The name *Johnny Cake* is a corruption of *Journey Cake* for this simple corn meal dish was probably first used by the pioneers when on journeys to frontiers, wars or hunts. Served with fresh country butter, piping hot off the griddle (one person has to stand and fry while the rest eat, and of course you have to eat near the stove), you can't beat this simple concoction for the full-bodied flavor of the stone ground corn meal. If you want to be literal and cook the daubs of batter on a hoe or shovel over a campfire, you will have Hoe Cake.

Hush Puppies

2 CUPS CORN MEAL   I ONION CHOPPED
I TEASPOON SALT   I EGG BEATEN
½ TEASPOON SODA   2 CUPS MILK
I TEASPOON CREAM OF TARTAR

Mix together the dry ingredients with chopped onion. Add beaten egg, combined with milk, and beat until smooth. You should have a thick mixture which can be formed into oblong shapes or dropped from a spoon. Brown these on both sides in plenty of fat using the same dish in which fish has been fried. These are always eaten at southern fish fries.

Luncheon & Supper Dishes

Wheat Waffles

I ½ CUPS WHEAT FLOUR
¾ TEASPOON SALT
2 TEASPOONS BAKING POWDER
2 TABLESPOONS BROWN SUGAR

2 EGGS
I ¼ CUPS MILK
5 TABLESPOONS MELTED SHORTENING

Sift the wheat flour, measure, add salt, and baking powder. Separate eggs and beat yolks until light. Add milk, sugar and slightly cooled shortening. Sift in the wheat flour mixture and stir quickly just enough to dampen the flour. Beat egg whites until stiff, but not dry. Fold into the batter as quickly as possible, stirring no more than necessary. Cook in hot waffle iron until crisp and brown. Serve with Vermont maple syrup or honey.

Corn Meal Waffles

1 CUP CORN MEAL	1 ½ CUPS MILK
1 CUP WHEAT FLOUR	¼ CUP MELTED SHORTENING
2 TEASPOONS BAKING POWDER	3 EGG YOLKS, WELL BEATEN
½ TEASPOON SALT	3 EGG WHITES, STIFFLY BEATEN
3 TABLESPOONS HONEY	

Sift wheat flour, measure, add corn meal, baking powder and salt and sift again. Add egg yolks combined with milk, honey, and shortening. Fold in egg whites. Bake on hot waffle iron and serve with Vermont maple syrup or honey.

Polenta

1 CUP CORN MEAL	¾ TEASPOON SALT
3 CUPS BOILING WATER	¼ POUND GRATED ROMA OR
1 EGG, WELL BEATEN	PROVOLONI CHEESE (ABOUT 1 CUP)

This grand old Italian dish is used widely in America by all races because it is so different.

Stir corn meal into salted water and cook until thick. Remove from fire. Add cheese, stirring until it is all melted, then add beaten egg. Drop by tablespoonfuls on cookie sheet. When cold, brown the cakes in butter on a hot griddle.

Serve plain with butter or with your favorite tomato sauce.

Roast Meat

Any cut of meat suitable for roasting may be rubbed with salt and pepper, and dredged with wheat flour. Pat on 1 teaspoon Worcestershire sauce with fingertips, sprinkle with a mixture of herbs, lay slices of onion over all and bake or pot-roast in the usual manner.

Baked or Fried Fish

Any fish suitable for frying or baking may be rolled in either stone ground corn meal or stone ground wheat flour.

Meat Wheat Casserole

1 CUP CRACKÉD WHEAT CEREAL (UNCOOKED)	2 CUPS TOMATOES
1 L.B. HAMBURG	2 TABLESPOONS CATSUP
½ ONION, CHOPPED	1 TEASPOON SALT
½ CUP BOILING WATER	1 TEASPOON POULTRY SEASONING
	1 TEASPOON WORCESTERSHIRE
	DASH OF PEPPER

Saute onions and meat in some fat until brown. Pour the boiling water over the cereal and add to the meat. Add the other ingredients and mix thoroughly. Place in a greased casserole and bake at 325° for about 1 hour.

Chicken-Corn Meal Casserole

1 CUP CORN MEAL	1 ½ TEASPOONS SALT
3 CUPS CHICKEN BROTH	1 TEASPOON BAKING POWDER
3 EGG YOLKS	2 TABLESPOONS BUTTER
3 EGG WHITES	1 CUP COOKED CHICKEN, CHOPPED

Pour hot chicken broth over the corn meal and stir until smooth. Cook until thick, stirring to prevent lumps. Remove from fire, add butter and stir until melted.

Beat egg yolks and add to the mixture, then add salt, baking powder and chicken. Fold in beaten egg whites. Pour into a buttered casserole and bake 1 hour at 325°. Serve hot.

Corn Meal-Beef Casserole

1 ½ CUPS BEEF STOCK	2 TABLESPOONS FAT
½ CUP CORN MEAL	⅔ CUP CHOPPED COOKED BEEF
SALT TO TASTE	1 EGG, BEATEN
½ ONION	TOMATOES, SLICED

Cook corn meal in beef stock until thick. Add more salt if necessary. Brown the chopped onion in the fat and add to corn meal mixture with the beef. Add beaten egg last.

Arrange in buttered casserole with alternate layers of sliced tomato.

Bake at 350° for 20 minutes.

Salmon Loaf

1 CAN SALMON	1 TABLESPOON CHOPPED PARSLEY
½ CUP SAMP CEREAL	2 EGG YOLKS
1 CUP MILK	2 EGG WHITES
4 TABLESPOONS MELTED BUTTER	1 TEASPOON WORCESTERSHIRE
¾ TEASPOON SALT	SAUCE

Cook the samp in milk for 10 minutes. Add flaked salmon, butter, salt and parsley and mix together well. Then add beaten egg yolks and Worcestershire sauce. Fold in the beaten egg whites and pour the mixture into a buttered casserole. Cover with whole wheat bread crumbs. Set the dish in a pan of hot water and bake 30 minutes in moderately hot oven. Any leftover portions are delicious sliced and browned in butter in a frying pan.

This may also be made with tuna fish.

Creamed Lobster

1 ½ CUPS MILK	½ CAN LOBSTER
3 TABLESPOONS WHEAT FLOUR	¼ TEASPOON WORCESTERSHIRE
4 TABLESPOONS COLD WATER	SAUCE
¾ TEASPOON SALT	ONION JUICE TO FLAVOR

Combine the wheat meal, water and salt and add to the hot milk. Stir until thickened and the mixture comes to a boil. Add other ingredients and let it rest on back of the stove for about fifteen minutes, that the lobster flavor may permeate the whole thing.

Serve on split Vermont Crackers, warmed in the oven.

Desserts & Cereals

Steamed Indian Pudding

1 CUP CORN MEAL	½ TEASPOON SODA
⅛ CUP WHEAT FLOUR	1 QUART HOT MILK
1 TEASPOON CINNAMON	1 CUP COLD MILK
½ TEASPOON CLOVES	½ CUP MOLASSES
½ TEASPOON NUTMEG	½ CUP MAPLE SYRUP
½ TEASPOON SALT	1 CUP CHOPPED SUET
1 CUP RAISINS	2 EGGS

Mix the corn meal with the cold milk and stir into the hot milk. Add the suet, molasses, and maple syrup. Beat the eggs until light and add to mixture. Then sift the wheat flour with the soda, spices and salt, mix with raisins, add to mixture and stir all well. Pour into a buttered mold. Cover tight and steam or cook in boiling water 4 hours. Be sure the water is kept boiling constantly and does not boil away.

Serve with hard sauce, whipped cream or any steamed pudding sauce. The pudding may be heated over in the oven making it as fresh and delicious as when it comes from the steaming mold.

Vermont Indian Pudding

7 TABLESPOONS CORN MEAL	½ TEASPOON SALT
I QUART MILK, SCALDED	½ TEASPOON CINNAMON
⅓ CUP MOLASSES	½ TEASPOON NUTMEG
⅓ CUP MAPLE SYRUP	

Stir corn meal into scalded milk. Add rest of ingredients. Mix well and turn into buttered casserole. Place in pan of hot water and bake, without stirring, in moderate oven for 3 hours or more. If you want whey, you must be sure and pour in a little cold milk, after it is all mixed.

Baked Indian Pudding with Suet

I QUART MILK	½ TEASPOON GINGER
½ CUP CORN MEAL	½ TEASPOON NUTMEG
¾ CUP BROWN SUGAR	I TEASPOON CINNAMON
I TEASPOON SALT	½ CUP RAISINS
I TEASPOON SODA	¼ CUP SUET, CUT FINE

Scald 3 cups of the milk. Add all other ingredients. Bake 10 minutes in a hot oven. Lower temperature to 300°, stir with a spoon, pour the cup of cold milk on top and bake 1 hour or more.

Samp Indian Pudding

½ CUP SAMP CEREAL, UNCOOKED	½ CUP CHOPPED NUTS
I QUART MILK	½ TEASPOON SALT
¼ CUP MOLASSES	¼ TEASPOON GINGER
⅓ CUP BROWN SUGAR	½ TEASPOON CINNAMON
½ CUP RAISINS	I TABLESPOON BUTTER

Scald the samp with milk. Add other ingredients, mix well and pour into buttered casserole or deep baking dish, cover and bake

3 hours at 250°, or set the dish in a pan of hot water and bake at 300°. Serve with boiled cider sauce made as follows:—

Boiled Cider Hard Sauce

1 CUP CONFECTIONER'S SUGAR
2 TABLESPOONS BUTTER
BOILED CIDER

Blend butter and sugar until crumbly. Then add just enough boiled cider to dampen the sugar. Beat until smooth, then place in the refrigerator until hard.

Any proportion of sugar and butter may be used and boiled cider added to make the sauce the consistency of a thick icing. There is no reason why this couldn't be used as an icing too . . . on the applesauce wheat cake, for instance.

Firmenty

½ CUP CRACKED WHEAT
1 CUP BOILING WATER
3 CUPS MILK
½ TEASPOON SALT
¼ TEASPOON GRATED NUTMEG
⅛ CUP MAPLE SUGAR
½ CUP RAISINS

Sprinkle cracked wheat into boiling water in top of double boiler, stirring until thickened. When water is absorbed add all other ingredients and steam in double boiler for three hours.

Serve hot with cream or top milk.

Steamed Oatmeal Pudding

¼ CUP BUTTER OR CHOPPED SUET, OR BOTH
½ CUP MOLASSES
1 CUP HOT BUTTERMILK
1 EGG, BEATEN
1½ CUPS SCOTCH OATMEAL
½ TEASPOON SODA
1 TEASPOON SALT
1 CUP RAISINS AND CHOPPED DATES

Crush soda in the palm of your hand and add to the oatmeal and salt. Cut suet or butter into the mixture with a knife. Add hot buttermilk and molasses, then beaten egg and mix well. Add raisins and dates last.

Put this batter into a buttered mold no more than ⅔ full, cover closely, place mold in another dish of boiling water, having the water come half way up on the mold. Steam 2 or 2½ hours adding hot water to the steamer as required.

Serve hot with Boiled Cider Hard Sauce or Steamed Pudding Sauce. This recipe makes a generous amount since it is poor economy to make a small amount in one steaming. However, the pudding is just as good, if not better, warmed in a strainer placed over boiling water for 10 or 15 minutes.

Mother's Suet Pudding

1 CUP SOUR MILK OR BUTTERMILK	1 TEASPOON SALT
1 CUP SUET, CHOPPED FINE	1 TEASPOON CINNAMON
1 CUP MOLASSES	¼ TEASPOON CLOVES
2½ CUPS WHEAT FLOUR	½ TEASPOON NUTMEG
1 TEASPOON SODA	1 CUP RAISINS

Mix together milk, suet and molasses. Sift wheat flour, measure, add other dry ingredients and sift into the batter. Mix well and add raisins.

Pour into a greased mold no more than ⅔ full. Cover closely and steam 3 hours with the water half way up on the mold. Or steam 2 hours in smaller containers.

Serve with Steamed Pudding Sauce.

Mother's Steamed Pudding Sauce

1 CUP SUGAR	2 TABLESPOONS BUTTER
3 TABLESPOONS CORNSTARCH	2 CUPS BOILING WATER
A LITTLE SALT	½ TEASPOON VANILLA

Mix together sugar, cornstarch and salt. Add the boiling water and cook until the sauce is clear, stirring to keep it smooth. Add butter and vanilla last.

Serve hot over steamed puddings.

Southern Souffle

½ CUP CORN MEAL	1½ CUPS MILK
⅛ TEASPOON SALT	GRATED RIND OF HALF LEMON
⅛ CUP SUGAR	4 EGG YOLKS
¼ CUP BUTTER	4 EGG WHITES

Here is a fine dish, equally good as a side dish or dessert. Scald milk and add 2 teaspoons of butter and the salt. Stir in corn meal and cook until the thick paste is smooth. Take off stove and cool. Now cream the rest of the butter with sugar and lemon rind and beat in egg yolks thoroughly. Add the cooled paste. Beat the egg whites until stiff and fold into the mixture. Put into a buttered pudding dish about a 2 inch thick layer of mixture and spread over it a coating of your favorite marmalade, then another layer of mixture and so on, having top layer that of the mixture. Bake about an hour or until done, in medium oven. You can serve wine sauce on it.

Corn Fritters

½ CUP CORN MEAL	I EGG YOLK
¼ CUP BREAD CRUMBS FINE	I EGG, WELL BEATEN
I TABLESPOON SUGAR	I TABLESPOON BUTTER
DASH OF SALT	I CUP MILK
I TEASPOON GRATED LEMON RIND	

Pour sugar and salt into milk and bring to boil in double boiler. Pour in corn meal slowly, constantly stirring. Let it boil gently for 20 minutes. Take off fire and stir in the butter, lemon rind and egg yolk. Turn mixture out onto a dampened bread board, and flatten out about half-inch thick. Cool and cut into round or square pieces as suits your fancy, and dip into the beaten egg, then into bread crumbs. Cook in hot deep fat, until dark brown. Drain and serve with Vermont maple sugar or marmalade.

Pastry or Pie-Crust

I ½ CUPS WHEAT FLOUR	½ CUP LESS I TABLESPOON SHORT-
¾ TEASPOON SALT	ENING
½ TEASPOON BAKING POWDER	⅓ CUP COLD WATER

Sift the wheat meal, measure, add salt and baking powder and sift into mixing bowl. Blend in shortening with a pastry cutter. The mixture should hold together when pinched between fingertips. If it does not, add more shortening. Dampen with cold water from the tap. Do not use ice water. Mix to a dough. Sift a small amount of wheat flour over a pastry cloth using only enough barely to cover the cloth. Cut off enough dough to line a pie plate and roll out on cloth. Turn the pastry over frequently to keep from sticking. Roll as thin as possible and line the pie plate. Fill with any desired pie filling, roll out the upper crust in the same manner. Dampen the rim of the under crust with more cold water and press upper crust into place with a fork dipped in the wheat flour. Cut slits in upper crust before placing on pie. Trim both crusts and bake at 400° around 30 minutes. Bake longer if the filling requires it.

Shortcake

2 CUPS WHEAT FLOUR	4 TABLESPOONS SHORTENING
2 TABLESPOONS SUGAR	½ CUP MILK
3 TEASPOONS BAKING POWDER	½ CUP WATER
1 TEASPOON SALT	

Sift wheat meal, measure, add sugar, baking powder and salt, and sift again. Work shortening into dry mixture with a pastry cutter or finger tips. Add liquid all at once, mix up quickly just enough to dampen the dry mixture thoroughly. Spread in round or square cake pan. Bake in hot oven about 15 minutes. When done, cut into squares, or any desired shape, split open, spread with butter and cover with any desired berry or fruit mixture.

Date Bars

¾ CUP WHEAT FLOUR	¼ CUP SHORTENING
¼ TEASPOON BAKING POWDER	2 EGGS, BEATEN
½ TEASPOON SALT	1 CUP DATES
1 CUP SUGAR	¾ CUP CHOPPED WALNUTS OR PECANS

Blend shortening into the sugar and add the beaten eggs. Sift the wheat flour, measure, add baking powder and salt and sift again into the batter. Put the dates and nuts on top, then mix all together and beat for one minute with a spoon. Spread in well-greased, wheat-floured 8 x 8 inch pan. Bake 15 or 20 minutes at 350°. Cut in any desired shape while still warm.

Brownies

2 SQUARES CHOCOLATE MELTED WITH
½ CUP BUTTER OR OTHER SHORTEN-
ING
2 EGGS, BEATEN
1 CUP SUGAR

¾ CUP WHEAT FLOUR
½ TEASPOON BAKING POWDER
½ TEASPOON SALT
½ CUP CHOPPED WALNUTS
1 TEASPOON VANILLA

Beat eggs, add sugar, chocolate mixture and vanilla and beat with a spoon. Sift the wheat flour, measure, add baking powder and salt, sift into batter and mix well. Add nuts and beat one minute with a spoon. Pour into shallow pan and bake 15 to 20 minutes at 350°. Cut in squares while warm.

English Fruit Cake

½ POUND BUTTER
½ POUND BROWN SUGAR
8 EGGS, SEPARATED
1 ½ CUPS WHEAT FLOUR
1 TEASPOON CINNAMON
1 TEASPOON ALLSPICE
1 TEASPOON CLOVES
1 TEASPOON NUTMEG
½ TEASPOON MACE
TRACE OF GINGER

¼ CUP BRANDY OR RUM
1 POUND SEEDLESS RAISINS
1 POUND CURRANTS
½ CUP CITRON
1 CUP LEMON PEEL
1 CUP ORANGE PEEL
½ POUND DATES
1 CUP CHOPPED NUTS
½ CUP SIFTED WHEAT FLOUR

Cream the butter with brown sugar. Beat the egg yolks and mix thoroughly with the sugar and butter.

Sift the wheat flour, measure, add spices and sift into the sugar mixture. Mix well and add the brandy or rum. Add the half cup of sifted wheat flour to the fruit and nuts and add to the batter, mixing thoroughly.

Beat the egg whites until stiff but not dry and fold into the mixture.

Pour into well greased, wheat floured dishes filling them no more than ⅔ full. Tie waxed paper over the top and bake at 300° for 3 hours with a large pan of hot water placed in the bottom of the oven. The top of the cake should burst open when done.

Maple Sugar Cake

I CUP SOFT MAPLE SUGAR
   (8 OUNCES)
¼ CUP SHORTENING
I EGG, WELL BEATEN
⅔ CUP MILK

I ¾ CUP WHEAT FLOUR
½ TEASPOON SALT
2 TEASPOONS BAKING POWDER
I CUP CHOPPED NUTS (OPTIONAL)

Blend shortening and maple sugar until smooth. If the sugar is lumpy place over hot water for a few minutes to soften. Add the beaten egg and beat all together well. Add the milk. Sift the wheat flour, measure, add salt and baking powder and sift into the batter. Add the chopped nuts. Beat all together for one minute. Bake in 2 layers 15 to 20 minutes at 350°.

MAPLE FROSTING:—Boil 1 cup of maple syrup, or 1 cup of maple sugar plus ¼ cup boiling water, until it will spin a thread. Pour syrup gradually over 2 beaten egg whites, beating constantly. Continue beating until thick enough to spread on a cake and have it stay there.

Sour Cream Devil's Food Cake

⅛ CUP SHORTENING
I ¼ CUPS SUGAR
I EGG, UNBEATEN
3 SQUARES MELTED CHOCOLATE
I TEASPOON VANILLA

½ CUP THICK SOUR CREAM
I CUP SWEET MILK
I ¾ CUPS WHEAT FLOUR
I TEASPOON SODA
½ TEASPOON SALT

Cream the shortening, add sugar all at once and mix with a pastry blender, then beat with a spoon. Add the egg and beat thoroughly, then unsweetened chocolate and vanilla and beat again. Add sour cream and milk and mix until smooth.

Sift the wheat flour, measure, add soda and salt and sift again into the batter. Mix quickly until smooth, then beat with a spoon for one minute by the clock. Pour into 2 greased layer cake pans and bake at 350° about 30 minutes. Spread with any desired frosting.

Applesauce Wheat Cake

½ CUP SHORTENING
1 CUP SUGAR
1 CUP APPLESAUCE
1 ½ CUPS WHEAT FLOUR

1 TEASPOON SODA
1 TEASPOON CINNAMON
½ TEASPOON GROUND CLOVES
1 CUP RAISINS

Cream shortening, add sugar, mix and beat until smooth. Add applesauce and mix thoroughly. Sift wheat flour, measure, add soda and spices and sift into batter. Pour raisins on top of meal, mix all together and beat for 2 minutes. Bake in greased and wheat floured loaf cake pan for 35 to 40 minutes at 350°.

This recipe may also be baked as cupcakes.

Old English Drop Cookies

1 CUP BROWN SUGAR
½ CUP SHORTENING
1 EGG
½ CUP COLD COFFEE
½ TEASPOON CINNAMON
½ TEASPOON NUTMEG

½ TEASPOON SODA
¾ TEASPOON BAKING POWDER
¾ TEASPOON SALT
1 CUP WHEAT FLOUR
1 CUP RAISINS
½ CUP NUTS IF DESIRED

Mix in order given, beating egg into shortening and sugar mixture. Sift the wheat meal after measuring. Beat all together for one minute. Drop by spoonfuls on greased cookie sheet. Bake at 375° for 10 to 15 minutes.

Green Mountain Hermits

2 CUPS CORN MEAL
¼ CUP BUTTER
¼ CUP LARD
1 ½ CUPS BROWN SUGAR
2 EGGS

½ TEASPOON SODA
¾ TEASPOON SALT
1 TEASPOON CINNAMON
¼ TEASPOON CLOVES
⅓ CUP CHOPPED NUTS

Cream butter and lard together; add brown sugar in small amounts at a time. Then add the beaten eggs and beat well. Combine dry ingredients with the chopped nuts and add to first mixture,

beating well. Drop by teaspoonfuls on greased pan. Bake at 375°
until done. Cookies like these can't hurt the kids, even if they raid
the cookie jar and eat their fill.

Oatmeal Cookies

½ CUP HOT MILK	I EGG, WELL BEATEN
I CUP SCOTCH OATMEAL	I CUP WHEAT FLOUR
¼ CUP MELTED SHORTENING	I ½ TEASPOONS BAKING POWDER
¾ CUP BROWN SUGAR	½ TEASPOON SALT
	½ TEASPOON CINNAMON

Pour hot milk over the oatmeal and add the hot shortening. Mix
well and add the sugar, then the beaten egg.

Sift the wheat flour, measure, add baking powder, salt and cinnamon. Sift into the batter, mix thoroughly and drop by spoonfuls
on a greased cookie sheet. Bake at 375° for 10 to 15 minutes. One-
half cup of nuts and ½ cup of seedless raisins may be added if desired or used for decoration.

Apple Crunch

2 CUPS SLICED RAW APPLES	½ CUP SUGAR
½ CUP RAISINS OR DATES	½ TEASPOON SALT
⅓ CUP BUTTER OR OTHER SHORTEN-	I CUP WHEAT FLOUR
ING	NUTMEG OR CINNAMON

Put apples and other fruit in buttered casserole. Mix together
butter, flour, salt and sugar. Spread on top of fruit and sprinkle
with nutmeg or cinnamon. Bake 30 minutes at 400° and serve with
hard sauce or cream.

Corn Meal Gingerbread

I CUP CORN MEAL	I CUP SOUR MILK OR BUTTERMILK
½ CUP WHEAT FLOUR	½ CUP MOLASSES
½ TEASPOON SALT	4 TABLESPOONS SHORTENING
I TEASPOON SODA	I EGG
I TEASPOON GINGER	

Heat the molasses; stir in the corn meal, shortening, salt and ginger; cool. Add the milk. Sift the wheat flour, measure, add soda and sift into batter. Add well beaten egg, then mix and beat thoroughly. Pour into a shallow baking pan and bake 25 to 30 minutes in a moderately hot oven. Serve with whipped cream.

Corn Meal Mush

Today (our grandmother used an iron kettle), we put three cups of cold water in the upper part of a double-boiler, add a scant teaspoon of salt and one cup of corn meal and stir together. Set the mush over the boiling water in the double boiler and let it cook for an hour or two. If you have one of those heavy waterless aluminum or copper cookers, they work very well for making mush. Let it simmer over the lowest possible heat and the mush will cook in twenty minutes or a half hour.

Of course any leftover mush may be sliced and browned in butter in the frying pan and then eaten with butter and maple syrup or honey.

The simplest and earliest use of corn meal was to make that famous dish called *Corn Meal Mush*, or *Hasty Pudding*. You put some water into an iron kettle, got it boiling briskly and then stirred in corn meal with a dash of salt until it was thick. Then you cooked it, stirring all the while. This was used by all good old New England families as a breakfast cereal or a supper dish, with cream and maple syrup poured over it. If there was any left over, after it had cooled it was sliced and fried on a hot griddle and served doused with butter and Vermont maple syrup.

Cracked Wheat, Crushed Wheat, Samp Cereal
Scotch Oatmeal Cereal

I CUP CEREAL
I TEASPOON SALT
3 CUPS WATER

To save time, these cereals can be cooked the night before you want to eat them. In the upper part of your double boiler put the cereal, salt and boiling water and stir with a spoon. Cover and cook from ½ to I hour. Then turn off the heat and let the cereal remain over the hot water until morning when you will reheat and serve. This makes four generous servings or six moderate servings.

If you want to stand by and stir, you can cook all these whole grain cereals in about 20 to 25 minutes directly over the heat without a double-boiler, but you must keep stirring the mixture to prevent sticking and burning down.

You will also find, as we have, that there are all manner of delectable combinations to be made with the different cereals, by mixing them, or by adding raisins, prunes, nuts, and other things that are good to eat.

A word of explanation regarding Samp Cereal and Cracked Wheat Cereal. No matter how long you cook them they will never become a gooey soft cereal, but on the contrary, a cereal that is composed of particles like steamed rice, and therefore something that can be chewed.

The original Samp was the name originally given by the Massachusetts Indians to a native corn they pounded into coarse meal with a pestle and mortar, said mortar being a hollowed-out tree stump and said pestle being a large wooden club hitched to a bent-over sapling to lift it up. Samp mortars could be heard up and down Cape Cod and Long Island so that fog-bound sailors often found their way home on the Samp sound beam!

Samp cereal is coarsely ground corn and wheat, blended.

Index

Apple Crunch	60
Baked & Fried Fish	48
Batter Cakes	44

Biscuit

Baking Powder	39
Hush Puppies	46
Rye	40
Sour Cream	40

Bread

Buckwheat Hot Bread	33
Buttermilk Quick Bread	26
Cottage Loaf	20
Hot Bread	25
Muffin Meal	25
Oatmeal	22
Pumpernickle	21
Rye	20
Rye & Wheat	22
Salt-Rising	19
Wholegrain Basic	18

Brown Bread

Boston	32
Molasses	26
Quick	30
Sour Milk	32
Steamed Brown Bread	26
Sweet Milk	32
Brownies	57

Cake

Applesauce	59
Devil's Food	58
Fruit	57
Maple Sugar	58

Cereals

Cornmeal Mush	61
Cracked Wheat	62
Crushed Wheat	62
Oatmeal	62
Samp	62
Coffee Cake	31

Cookies

Oatmeal	60
Old English	59
Hermits	59

Corn Bread

Corn & Wheat	29
Countryman's	28
Early American	29
Southern	29
Spoon	30
Suet	30
Chicken Casserole	49
Corn Dodgers	45
Corn Fritters	55
Corn Pone	45
Date Bars	56
Doughnuts	33
Dumplings	41
Gingerbread	60

Griddlecakes

Buckwheat, quick	42
Buckwheat, raised	43
Buckwheat-Rice	44
Buttermilk	27–42
Corn & Wheat	42
Jam	27
Kentucky Raised	44
Maple Sugar Buckwheat No. 1	43
Maple Sugar Buckwheat No. 2	43
Wheat	41
Hoe Cake	46

Indian Pudding

Firmenty	53
Samp	52
Steamed	51
Suet	52
Vermont Baked	52
Lobster Casserole	50
Meat Casserole	49

Muffins

Blueberry	36
Combination	36
Corn Gems	37
Corn & Rye	35
Corn & Wheat	35
Jam	37
Kernel Corn	37
Nut	36
Oatmeal	37
Raisin	36
Wheat	34
Wheat & Rye	36
Polenta	48

Popovers

Corn	38
Rye or Wheat	38
Pie Crust	55

Pudding

Oatmeal	53
Suet	54

Rolls

Buttermilk	23
French Brioche	24
Roast meat	48
Wheat	23
Salmon Loaf	50

Sauce

Boiled Cider	53
Steamed Pudding	54
Scones	40
Shortcake	56
Souffle	54

Waffles

Corn	48
Wheat	47
Yorkshire Pudding	31